Primary School
Chinese

with

Dalong, Xiaolong, Mike and Candy

Marcus Reoch and Anne Martin

Our book aims to encourage children to learn primary school Chinese with the emphasis on speaking, writing Chinese characters and having lots of fun!

In total there are ten chapters with each chapter introducing a key topic that is linked to a child's everyday life. Each chapter contains a certificate, a Great Wall Challenge and stickers to further reinforce the key learning points. There is also a CD of the sound recordings at the back of the book.

Marcus and Anne have written the book using the objectives of the Primary Languages Framework as a key reference tool. In addition, the vocabulary and sentence patterns follow the specifications for the The Independent Schools Examinations Board (ISEB) Certificate of Achievement.

Book 1 also includes a free login to **Primary School Chinese Online** - a webportal full of games and competitions based on what they have already learnt. Please go to *www.primaryschoolchinese.com* for registration.

CONTENTS

Let's meet our 2 Chinese dragons, Dàlóng and Xiǎolóng!

Dàlóng
Big Dragon

Xiǎolóng
Little Dragon

Now let's meet their 2 friends, Mike and Candy!

Mike

Candy

Let's learn the **4** Chinese sounds!

1st sound
is like
singing a song!

2nd sound
is like
climbing a ladder!

3rd sound
is like
being on a roller coaster!

4th sound
is like
falling over and saying 'ow'!

First words...

Zhōngwén	**Chinese**
lǎoshī	**teacher**

Greetings

nǐ hǎo	**hello**
zàijiàn	**goodbye**
xièxie	**thank you**

Nǐ hǎo ma?	**How are you?**
Wǒ hěn hǎo.	**I am well.**

'a' sounds

Mā	**Mum**
chá	**tea**
mǎ	**horse**
dà	**big**

What language are we going to learn?

Zhōngwén
Chinese

Who is going to teach us?

lǎoshī
teacher

Say hello in Chinese!

nǐ hǎo

hello

Say goodbye in Chinese!

zàijiàn

goodbye

Join the red stars to see the word!

Join the blue dots to see the word!

Let's learn how to say thank you in Chinese!

xièxie

thank you

How do you say 'How are you'? and... 'I am well'?

Nǐ hǎo ma?

How are you?

Wǒ hěn hǎo.

I am well.

A-maze! Find your way out of the maze and say the words that you pass on the way to teacher!

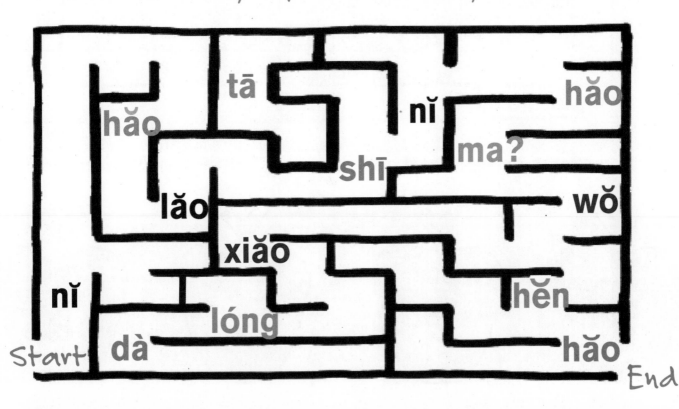

Let's learn some 'a' sounds in Chinese!

ā   **á**   **ă**   **à**

Let's learn some 'a' words in Chinese!

Mā	chá	mă	dà
Mum	tea	horse	big

Practise some 'a' sounds with your classmates!

à   ā   á   ă

Let's write **big** and **small** in Chinese characters!

大
dà
big

小
xiǎo
small

Let's write **good** in Chinese characters!

woman

女

+

子

 =

child

好

hǎo
good

Draw the Chinese characters below!

dà

big

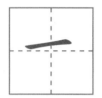   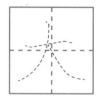

xiǎo

small

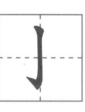 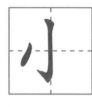 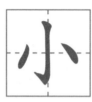  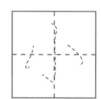

hǎo

good

=
     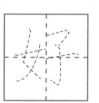

Help Dàlóng finish
writing 大 in the box.

Help Xiǎolóng finish
writing 小 in the box.

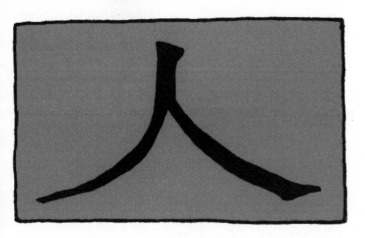

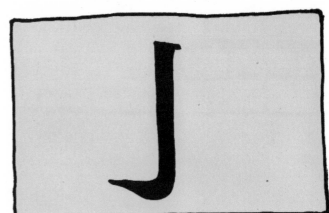

Colour in this **happy** Chinese character in
red, **blue**, yellow and **green**!

12

What have you learnt in
Chapter 1?

1

dà

mā

chá

mǎ

lǎoshī

Match the correct stickers to the Chinese words!

Congratulations, you have completed Chapter 1

Your name:_____

Now I can...

 say *hello* and *goodbye* in Chinese.

 say *thank you* in Chinese.

 say '*How are you?*' and '*I am well*' in Chinese.

 say 4 different 'a' sounds in Chinese.

say *big*, *small* and *good* in Chinese characters.

Let's go and learn more Chinese in Chapter 2!

I, you, he/she, we

wǒ	**I**
nǐ	**you**
tā	**he/she**
wǒmen	**we**

Nǐ jiào shénme? What's your name?

Wǒ jiào Max. I am called Max.

Numbers 1-5

yī	**1**
èr	**2**
sān	**3**
sì	**4**
wǔ	**5**

'e' sounds

chē	**car**
shé	**snake**
kě	**thirsty**
è	**hungry**

How do you say I, you, he and she in Chinese?

wǒ

I

nǐ
you

tā
he/she

How do you say we in Chinese?

wǒmen
we

Let's play 'Link'. Link the English to the Chinese by drawing a line between the correct words.

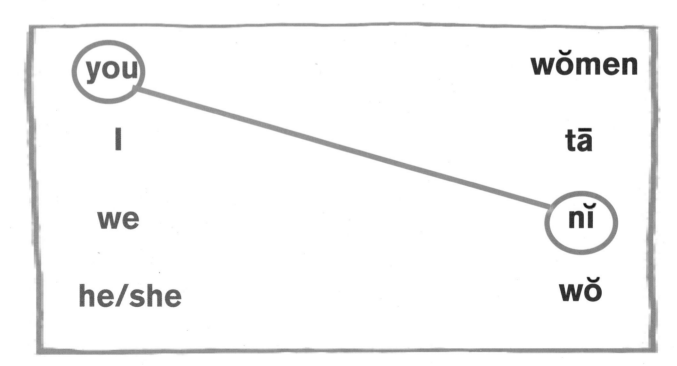

you   wǒmen

I   tā

we   nǐ

he/she   wǒ

How do you ask 'What's your name' in Chinese?

Nǐ jiào shénme?

What's your name?

How do you **say your name** in Chinese?

Wǒ jiào Mike.

Wǒ jiào Candy.

My name is Mike.

My name is Candy

Colour in the pictures and answer the questions!

Tā jiào shénme?

Tā jiào shénme?

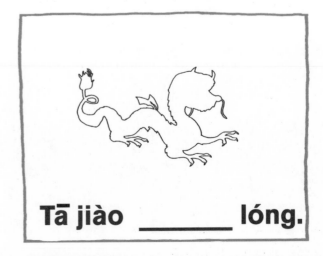

Tā jiào _____ lóng.

Tā jiào _____ lóng.

Let's learn how to say 1-5 in Chinese!

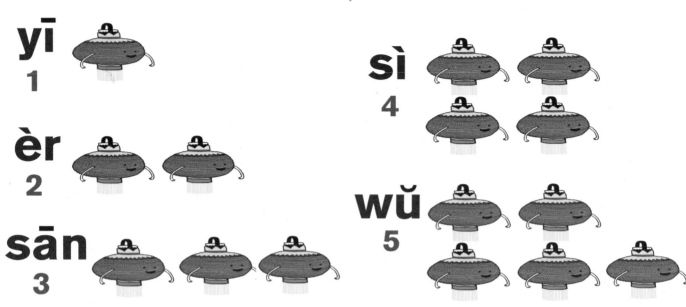

yī
1

èr
2

sān
3

sì
4

wŭ
5

How many? Write the answer in Chinese on the right!

Dàlóng	🐉	🐉	🐉			<u>sān</u>
Xiǎolóng	🐉					____
Candy	🚲	🚲				____
Mike	🧍	🧍	🧍	🧍	🧍	____
lǎoshī	👨‍🎓	👨‍🎓	👨‍🎓	👨‍🎓		____

Let's learn how to count 1-5 with our hands in Chinese!

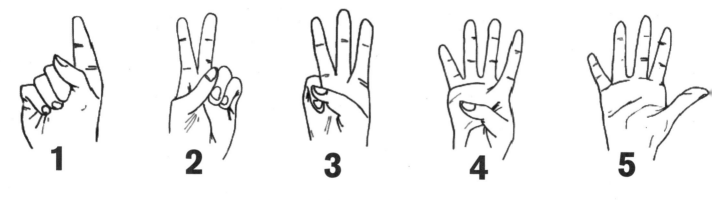

1   2   3   4   5

Let's learn some 'e' sounds in Chinese!

ē   é   ě   è

Let's learn some 'e' words in Chinese!

chē	shé	kě	è
car	snake	thirsty	hungry

Practise some 'e' sounds with your classmates!

é   ě   è   ē

Let's write numbers 1-5 in Chinese characters!

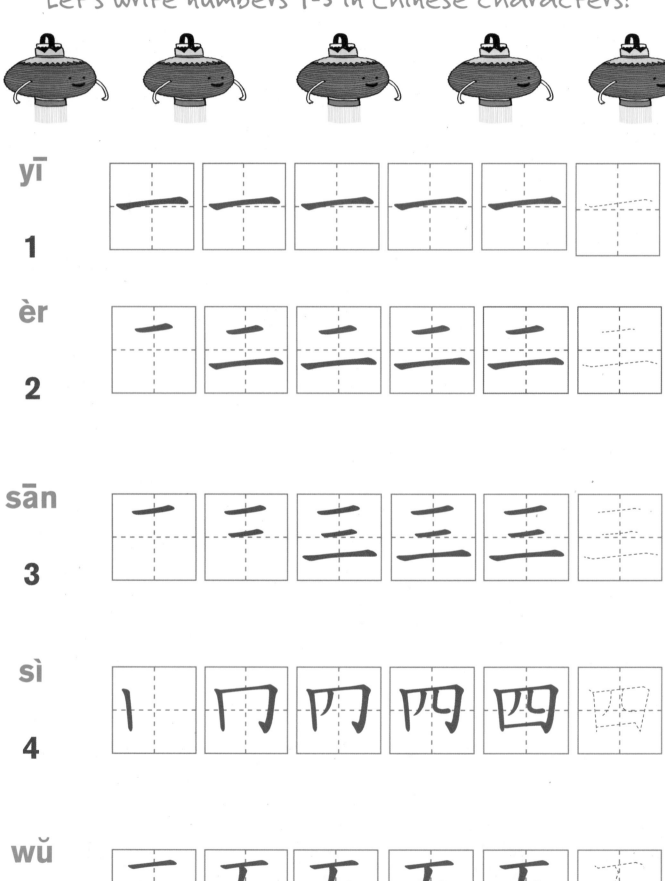

yī
1

èr
2

sān
3

sì
4

wǔ
5

Match the Chinese characters to the correct shapes and then colour in the pictures!

一 = **blue**

二 = **red**

三 = **yellow**

四 = **green**

五 = **black**

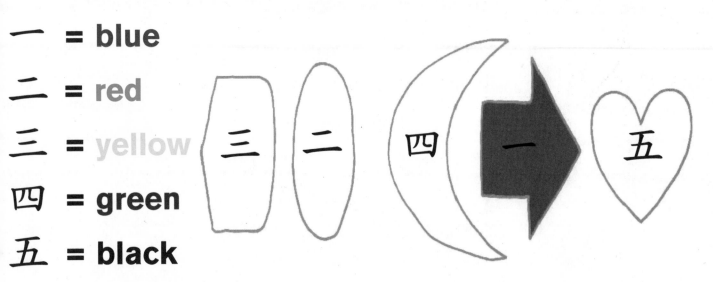

Number match! Colour in Mike and Candy using the correct colours!

一=**blue** 二=**pink** 三=**yellow** 四=**green** 五=**black**

What have you learnt in
Chapter 2?

1 **2**

dà	shé
mā	chē
chá	èr
mǎ	è
lǎoshī	kě

Match the correct stickers
to the Chinese words!

Congratulations, you have completed Chapter 2

Your name: _____

Now I can...

 say *I, you, he/she* and *we* in Chinese.

 count from *1 to 5* in Chinese.

 count from *1 to 5* in Chinese with my hands.

 say 4 different 'e' sounds in Chinese.

 write *1-5* in Chinese characters.

Let's go and learn more Chinese in Chapter 3!

Numbers 6-10

liù	**6**
qī	**7**
bā	**8**
jiǔ	**9**
shí	**10**

Nǐ jǐ suì?	**How old are you?**
Wǒ qī suì.	**I am 7 years old.**

'i' sounds

jī	**chicken**
lí	**pear**
mǐ	**rice**
qì	**angry**

Let's learn how to count from 6-10 in Chinese!

liù
6

qī
7

bā
8

jiǔ
9

shí
10

Count our friends and fill in the gaps in Chinese!

Candy <u>liù</u>

Mike _____

Xiǎolóng _____

lǎoshī _____

Dàlóng _____

How do you ask 'How old are you' in Chinese?

Nǐ jǐ suì ?

How old are you?

Now tell teacher how old you are in Chinese!

Wǒ bā suì.

Wǒ liù suì.

I am 8 years old.   I am 6 years old.

Light the correct number of candles to say the correct age!

Wǒ bā suì.

Nǐ liù suì.

Tā jiǔ suì.

Wǒmen qī suì.

Let's count 6-10 with our hands in Chinese!

6　　　**7**　　　**8**　　　**9**　　　**10**

'Hand Draw' - in the boxes below, carefully draw the hand signs for number 8 and number 9!

8　　　**9**

Let's learn some 'i' sounds in Chinese!

Let's learn some 'i' words in Chinese!

jī	lí	mǐ	qì
chicken	pear	rice	angry

Practise some 'i' sounds with your classmates!

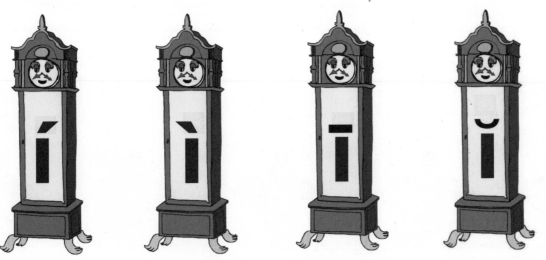

Let's write numbers 6-10 in Chinese characters!

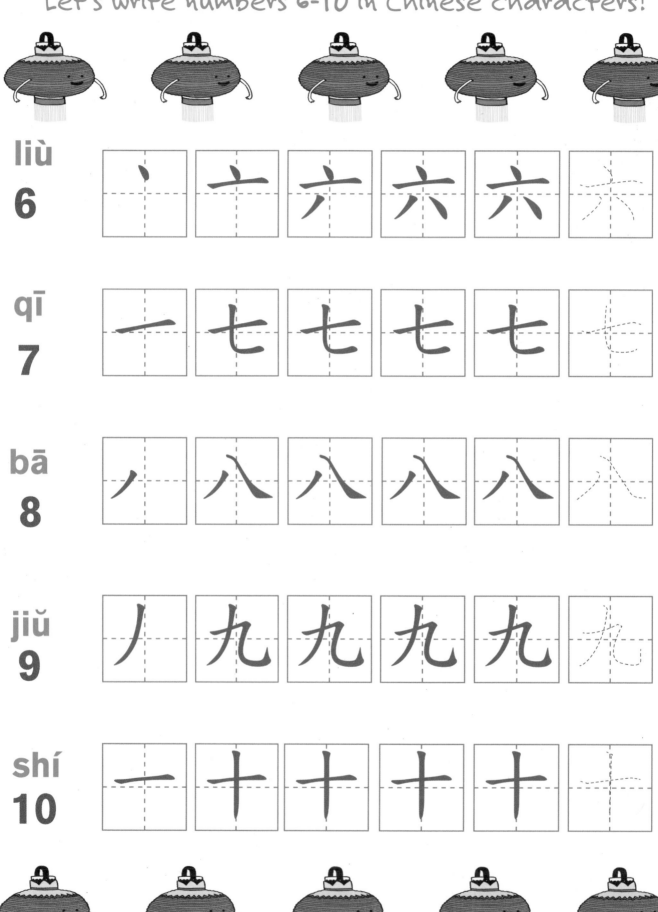

liù
6

qī
7

bā
8

jiǔ
9

shí
10

Help Mike and Candy find the **pairs** of Chinese characters. We have done 六 for you!

九	九	六	六	十
六	六	七	七	十
八	八	十	八	六
九	九	十	八	六
十	十	五	七	七

Let's play 'Number Map'. Help Dàlóng find the path from left to right for the 5 Chinese numbers!

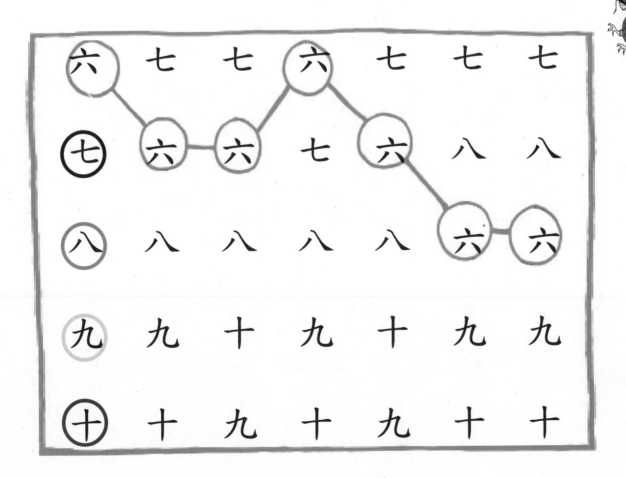

What have you learnt in Chapter 3?

1	2	3
dà	shé	liù
mā	chē	jī
chá	èr	lí
mǎ	è	mǐ
lǎoshī	kě	qì

Match the correct stickers to the Chinese words!

Congratulations, you have completed Chapter 3

Your name: _____

Now I can...

count from *6-10* in Chinese.

say *my age* in Chinese.

count from *6-10* in Chinese with my hands.

say 4 different 'i' sounds in Chinese.

write *6-10* in Chinese characters.

Let's go and learn more Chinese in Chapter 4!

The boys!

Bàba	**Dad**
gēge	**big brother**
dìdi	**little brother**

The girls!

Māma	**Mum**
jiějie	**big sister**
mèimei	**little sister**

Nǐ shì shéi?	**Who are you?**
Wǒ shì jiějie.	**I am big sister.**

'o' words

bō	**wave**
Fó	**Buddha**
wǒ	**I**
mò	**ink**

Let's meet the **male** family members!

Bàba

Dad

gēge

big brother

dìdi

little brother

Let's meet the **female** family members!

Māma

Mum

jiějie

big sister

mèimei

little sister

Follow the strings and complete the correct names of the panda family!

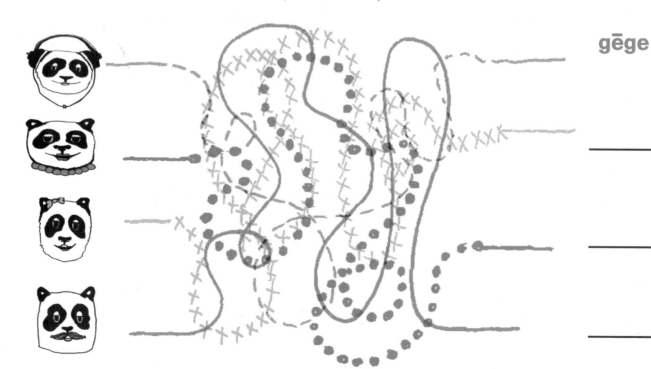

gēge

_____

_____

_____

Let's learn an important word in Chinese!

shéi?

who?

Who is little sister talking to?

 **Nǐ shì shéi?**

 **Wǒ shì dìdi.**

Who are you?   **I am little brother.**

Let's play 'Rock, Paper, Scissors'!

**Turn to your friend and say 'nǐ shì shéi?'
When you both say 'shéi', you must choose to
be a rock, paper or scissors. Who won?!**

```
U U J S J I E J I E
M I B E E W D I D I
D L A M E I M E I U
G E G E Z U I J U Z
L K F T O K G B L J
A D I E N S P I E Y
O D J L A U H B G Z
S F H D S L E I J C
H M A M A G D H S D
I B A B A F E G O K
```

Can you find the panda family hidden in the grid?

Bàba	**Māma**
gēge	**jiějie**
dìdi	**mèimei**

Now find the word for 'teacher' in Chinese!

Let's find out how old big sister is!

Nǐ jǐ suì?   **Wǒ bā suì.**

How old are you?   **I am 8 years old.**

Look at the panda family's tummies and write how old they are in Chinese in the gaps!

Wǒ bā suì.

Wǒ ___ suì.

Wǒ ___ suì.

Wǒ ___ suì.

Let's learn some 'o' sounds in Chinese

ō ó ǒ ò

Let's learn some 'o' words in Chinese!

bō	Fó	wǒ	mò
wave	Buddha	I	ink

Practise some 'o' sounds with your classmates!

Let's write Mum and Dad in Chinese!

Māma

Mum

Bàba

Dad

Spot the difference! Help Mike complete the incomplete characters on the right!

Let's learn the Chinese characters for the other members of the family!

哥哥 弟弟 姐姐 妹妹

| big brother | little brother | big sister | little sister |

Family ties! Can you help the panda family find their Chinese characters? Look, little brother has found his!

 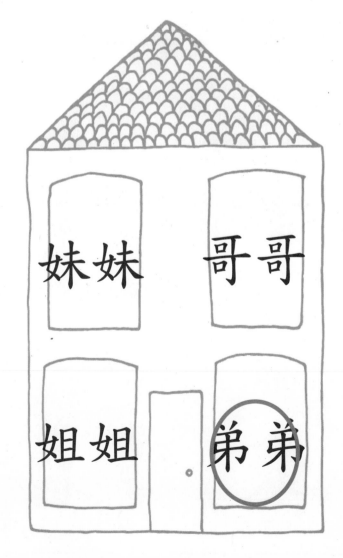

What have you learnt in Chapter 4?

1	2	3	4
dà	shé	liù	mò
mā	chē	jī	Fó
chá	èr	lí	bō
mǎ	è	mǐ	Māma
lǎoshī	kě	qì	Bàba

Match the correct stickers to the Chinese words!

 Congratulations, you have completed Chapter 4.

Your name:_____

Now I can...

say the members of *my family* in Chinese.

find out *who* people are in Chinese.

say 4 different 'o' sounds in Chinese.

write *Mum* and *Dad* in Chinese characters.

recognise 4 more *my family* Chinese characters.

Let's go and learn more Chinese in Chapter 5!

Countries

Zhōngguó	China
Yīngguó	England
Měiguó	America
Fǎguó	France

Cities

Lúndūn	London
Běijīng	Beijing

Nǐ zhù zài nǎlǐ?	Where do you live?
Wǒ zhù zài Zhōngguó.	I live in China.

'u' sounds

zhū	pig
zhú	bamboo
shǔ	mouse
lù	deer

Let's learn the names of 4 countries in Chinese!

Zhōngguó

China

Yīngguó

England

Měiguó

America

Fǎguó

France

Which country? Colour in the flags with the correct colours and then fill in the gaps below!

Yīngguó

Let's learn an important question word in Chinese!

nǎlǐ?

where?

Where does Candy live?

Nǐ zhù zài nǎlǐ?

Where do you live?

Wǒ zhù zài Yīngguó.

I live in England.

Which country? Mike lives in England - what about his friends...which countries do they live in?

 zhù zài  **Yīngguó** _____

 zhù zài  _____

 zhù zài  _____

 **zhù zài**  _____

Who lives where? Tell lǎoshī the answer in Chinese!
Look, we have done one for you:- 'Monkey **zhù zài** jungle!'

Fish	Dog
Horse	(Monkey)

zhù zài

Stable	Sea
Kennel	(Jungle)

Which country does Dàlóng live in?

Nǐ zhù zài nǎlǐ?

Wǒ zhù zài Zhōngguó.

Where do you live?   **I live in China.**

What are the capitals of China and England in Chinese?

Běijīng  **Beijing**   **Lúndūn** **London**

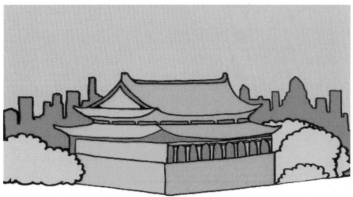

Let's learn some 'u' sounds in Chinese!

ū ú ǔ ù

Let's learn some 'u' words in Chinese!

zhū	zhú	shǔ	lù
pig	bamboo	mouse	deer

Practise some 'u' sounds with your classmates!

ǔ ú ū ù

Let's learn how to write China and Beijing in Chinese!

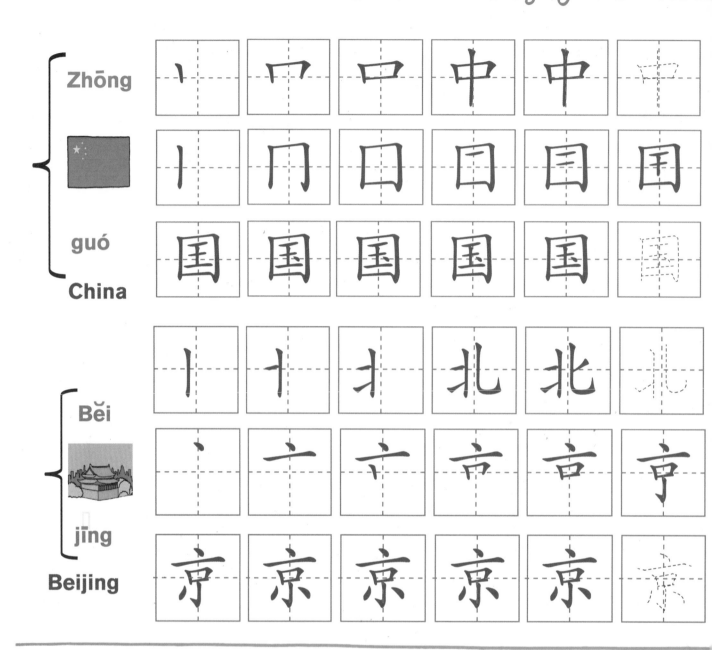

Zhōng
guó
China

Běi
jīng
Beijing

Number match! Colour in Beijing using the correct colours

一 = **blue**

二 = **red**

三 = **orange**

四 = **green**

Let's find out more about China!

Let's go travelling! How many Chinese characters can you find? Write the answers in Chinese in the gaps!

中 = sì   国 = ____   北 = ____   京 = ____

What have you learnt in Chapter 5?

1	2	3	4	5
dà	shé	liù	mò	lù
mā	chē	jī	Fó	zhū
chá	èr	lí	bō	Měiguó
mǎ	è	mǐ	Māma	zhú
lǎoshī	kě	qì	Bàba	shǔ

Match the correct stickers to the Chinese words!

Congratulations, you have completed Chapter 5.

Your name: _____

Now I can...

say *China, England, America* and *France* in Chinese.

say *Beijing* and *London* in Chinese.

say where *I live* in Chinese.

say 4 different 'u' sounds in Chinese.

write *China* and *Beijing* in Chinese characters.

Let's go and learn more Chinese in Chapter 6!

School things

bāo	bag
shū	book
chǐ	ruler
bǐ	pen

This and that

zhè	this
nà	that

zhè shì	this is
nà shì	that is

Colours

hóng	red
lǜ	green
lán	blue

Let's see what is in Mike's school bag!

bāo  bag

chǐ  ruler

shū  book

bǐ  pen

Help Xiǎolóng draw the pictures for the words in the drawing. Remember, the answers are above!

Let's learn how to say this and that in Chinese!

zhè

this

nà

that

This or that? Look at panda playing football with his school things - draw a circle around zhè or nà!

zhè

this

nà

that

bag   =   zhè or (nà)
pen   =   zhè or nà
ruler   =   zhè or nà
book   =   zhè or nà

This is a book and that is a pen!

Zhè shì shū.

Nà shì bǐ.

This is a book.

That is a pen.

Let's learn red, green and blue in Chinese!

hóng red

lǜ green

lán blue

'Odd one out'! Circle the word that is the odd colour out of the 3 choices.

hóng	(sunshine)	stop sign	tomato
lǜ	trees	horse	plants
lán	whale	sea	lamp
hóng	fog	lips	rose

Our friends have lost their names, their school things and their colours! Can you help them find them?

```
F M I K E B U C A N D Y C H T
L P R R H O N G S E V K E C C
A F A U D A L O N G R J M H H
N U O H L O S H U T E L I M I
T S C T O R D B A O V E N R
Y I H E R L A N E R T I B B N
W L I N L U T R T T L G B L B
X I A O L O N G R L L S T B A
```

How fast can you say this?

Māma qí mǎ
Mǎ màn
Māma mà mǎ!

Mum is riding a horse
The horse is slow
Mum tells the horse off!

Let's learn how to write our school things in Chinese!

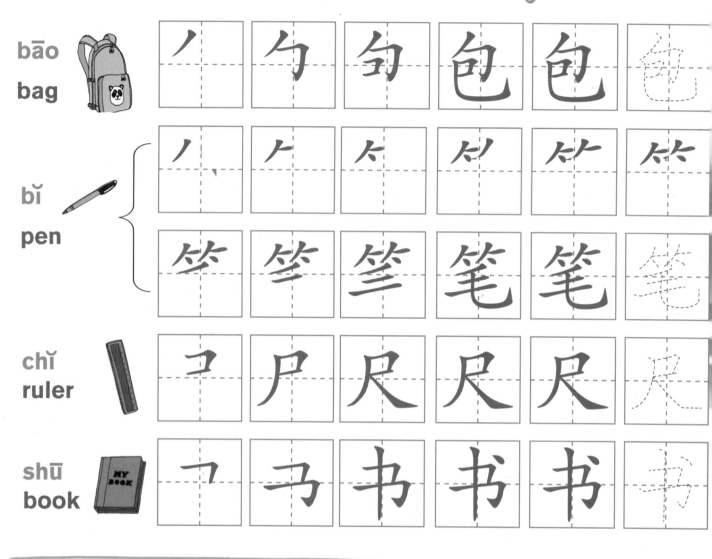

bāo
bag

bǐ
pen

chǐ
ruler

shū
book

How many school things can you find in Candy's bag?
Write the answers in Chinese!

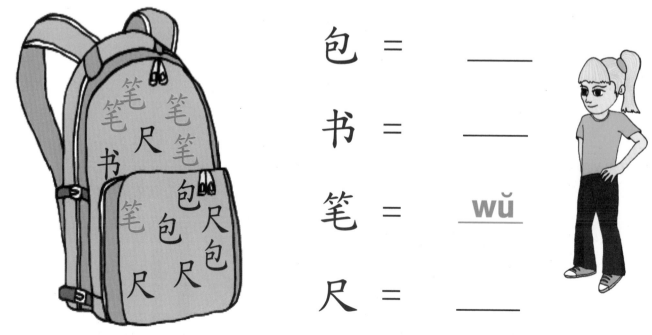

包 = ＿＿

书 = ＿＿

笔 = __wǔ__

尺 = ＿＿

Let's learn how to read red, green & blue in Chinese characters!

hóng    lǜ    lán

红   绿   蓝

Help Mike and Candy complete the Chinese characters!

hóng   **lǜ**

   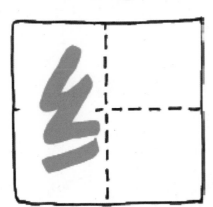   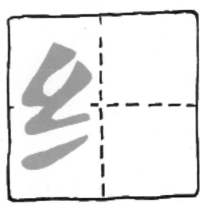   

Dàlóng is late for school! Help him match his school things wth the Chinese characters below!

红书   蓝包   绿笔   绿尺

What have you learnt in Chapter 6?

1	2	3	4	5
dà	shé	liù	mò	lù
mā	chē	jī	Fó	zhū
chá	èr	lí	bō	Měiguó
mǎ	è	mǐ	Māma	zhú
lǎoshī	kě	qì	Bàba	shǔ

Match the correct stickers to the Chinese words!

6

hóng

shū

lán

lǜ

bāo

Congratulations, you have completed Chapter 6

Your name:_____

Now I can...

say *bag, ruler, book* and *pen* in Chinese.

say *this* and *that* in Chinese.

say *this is* and *that is* in Chinese.

say *red, green* and *blue* in Chinese.

write *bag, ruler, book* and *pen* in Chinese characters

Let's go and learn more Chinese in Chapter 7!

Food

hànbǎobāo	hamburger
miàntiáo	noodles
pīsà	pizza

Drink

shuǐ	water
kělè	Coca Cola
chá	tea

Eat and Drink

chī	eat
hē	drink

Nǐ chī shénme?	What are you eating?
Nǐ hē shénme?	What are you drinking?

My favourite food is...?   My favourite drink is...?

hànbǎobāo

hamburger

miàntiáo

noodles

pīsà

pizza

shuǐ

water

kělè

Coca Cola

chá

tea

Draw it! What are all our friends having for lunch?
Can you draw what they are eating and drinking?

miàntiáo 	chá

pīsà	shuǐ 

hànbǎobāo	kělè

Let's learn how to say eat and drink in Chinese!

chī eat

hē drink

What is Dàlóng eating?

Wǒ chī pīsà.

I am eating pizza.

What is Candy drinking?

Wǒ hē kělè.

I am drinking Coca Cola.

Fill in the gaps with the food & drink that we have learnt this chapter. Write the answers in Chinese!

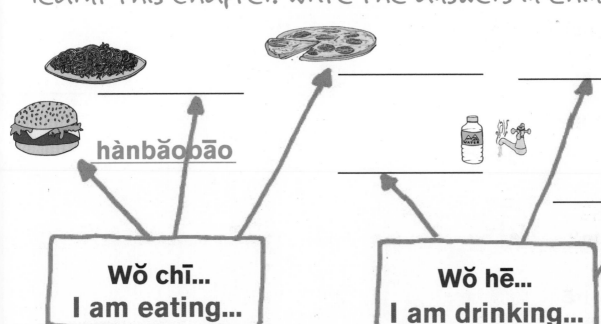

hànbǎobāo

Wǒ chī...
I am eating...

Wǒ hē...
I am drinking...

How do you ask 'What are you eating' in Chinese?

Nǐ chī shénme?

What are you eating?

How do you ask 'What are you drinking' in Chinese?

Nǐ hē shénme?

What are you drinking?

Look at the pictures, then follow the lines to work out what our friends are eating and drinking!

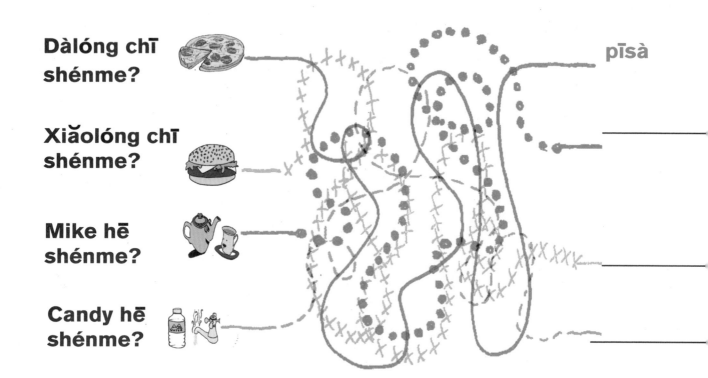

Dàlóng chī shénme?

Xiǎolóng chī shénme?

Mike hē shénme?

Candy hē shénme?

pīsà

_____

_____

_____

Chinese people use chopsticks to eat food...

Draw the noodles in the bowl!

Help Xiǎolóng find his way out of the maze to the bowl and chopsticks!

Let's learn how to write some useful
food & drink words in Chinese!

chī

eat

| ㇒ | 口 | 口 | 吖 | 吃 | 吃 |
| 吃 | 吃 | 吃 | 吃 | 吃 | 吃 |

hē

drink

| ㇒ | 口 | 口 | 口 | 呞 | 呞 |
| 呞 | 呞 | 喝 | 喝 | 喝 | 喝 |

shuǐ

water

| 亅 | 水 | 水 | 水 | 水 | 水 |

Hidden below is a Chinese character - can you help
Candy to find out which one it is? Clue: it's a drink!

红　　水　喝　喝　喝　吃
　吃　红　吃　水　哥　哥　　吃
喝　　红　喝　水　喝　　哥　水
　哥　　　水　　　　水水　水
　红　　　水　水　水　水水　红
　水水水水　水　水水水　吃
吃　　　　　水　　　水水水
　水水水水水　水　　　水
　　喝　红　水　水　吃哥　哥　吃
　　　　　水　水　红　哥喝喝
　　　　水水　吃

Let's write **hamburger** in Chinese characters!

hànbǎobāo 汉堡包

Find the pairs! Match the **coloured** shapes with the **black & white** shapes and then colour in!

干 勹 己 呆 彳 氵

呆 干 己 氵 勹 亻

Let's play 'Battleships'! Find the Chinese characters in the grid below and write the correct reference!

	A	B	C	D	E	F
1	哥	汉	水	笔	红	哥
2	堡	好	笔	红	尺	笔
3	好	水	尺	尺	包	好
4	好	尺	吃	哥	尺	红
5	哥	红	好	水	水	喝

Ship 1   汉   **B1**

Ship 2   堡   __

Ship 3   包   __

Ship 4   吃   __

Ship 5   喝   __

72

What have you learnt in Chapter 7?

1	2	3	4	5
dà	shé	liù	mò	lù
mā	chē	jī	Fó	zhū
chá	èr	lí	bō	Měiguó
mǎ	è	mǐ	Māma	zhú
lǎoshī	kě	qì	Bàba	shǔ

Match the correct stickers to the Chinese words!

6	7

hóng

hē

shū

pīsà

lán

chī

lù

shuǐ

bāo

kělè

Congratulations, you have completed Chapter 7

Your name: _____

Now I can...

 say *hamburger, noodles* and *pizza* in Chinese.

 say *water,* **Coca Cola** and *tea* in Chinese.

 say what *I am eating* in Chinese.

say what *I am drinking* in Chinese.

write *drink, eat* and *water* in Chinese characters.

Let's go and learn more Chinese in Chapter 8!

Face

yǎnjīng	eye
bízi	nose
ěrduo	ear
zuǐba	mouth

Body

gēbo	arm
shǒu	hand
jiǎo	foot
tuǐ	leg

Where and here

| nǎlǐ? | where? |
| zhèlǐ | here |

| Yǎnjīng zài nǎlǐ? | Where are your eyes? |
| Yǎnjīng zài zhèlǐ. | My eyes are here. |

Let's learn some parts of the face in Chinese!

yǎnjīng   eye

bízi   nose

ěrduo   ear

zuǐba   mouth

Meet Mr Face! Fill in the gaps with the missing parts of the face in Chinese!

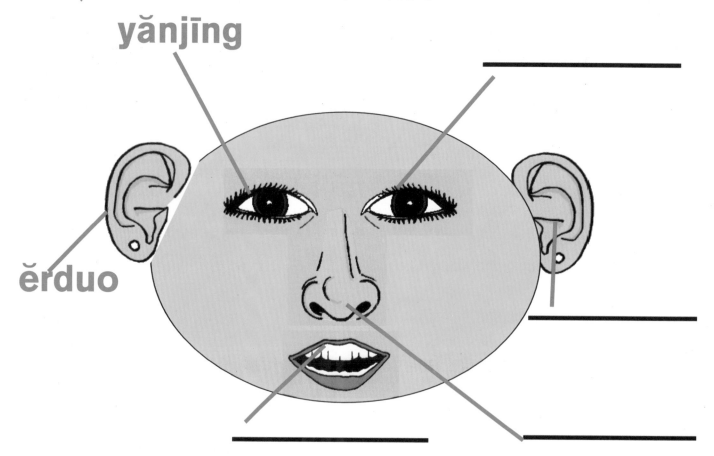

yǎnjīng

ěrduo

Let's learn some parts of the body in Chinese!

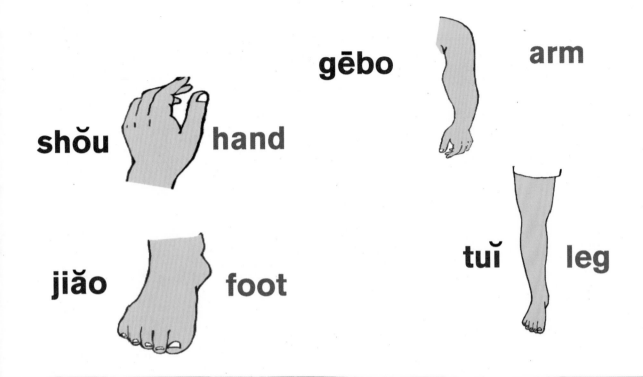

gēbo arm

shǒu hand

jiǎo foot

tuǐ leg

Meet Mrs Body! Fill in the gaps with the missing parts of the body in Chinese!

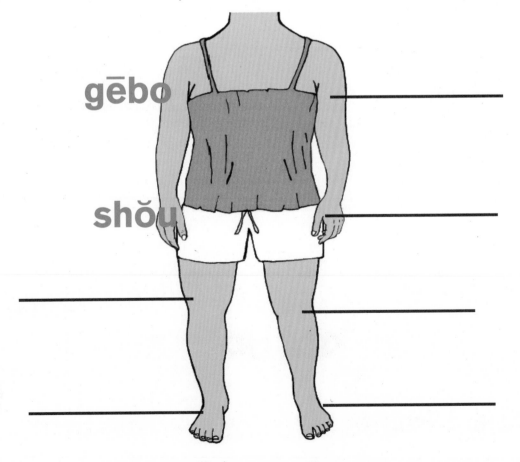

gēbo _____

shǒu _____

_____ _____

_____ _____

Help Xiǎolóng match up the face and body parts!

yǎnjīng

bízi

ěrduo

zuǐba

shǒu

jiǎo

Where?.......here!

nǎlǐ? **zhèlǐ**

where? here

Where are Mike's eyes?

Yǎnjīng zài nǎlǐ? Yǎnjīng zài zhèlǐ.

Where are your eyes? **My eyes are here.**

Help Candy fill in the answers in the puzzle below.
Choose the correct parts of the face & body in Chinese!

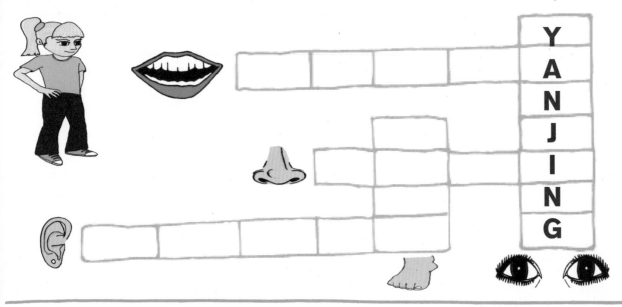

Where is Candy's foot?

Jiǎo zài nǎlǐ?

Jiǎo zài zhèlǐ.

Where is your foot?   **My foot is here.**

Meet my alien! Draw the correct number of face
and body parts on the alien!

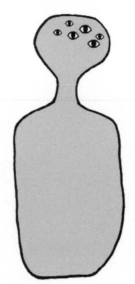

yǎnjīng	6
ěrduo	4
bízi	2
gēbo	4
tuǐ	3
jiǎo	6

Let's write **ear** and **hand** in Chinese!

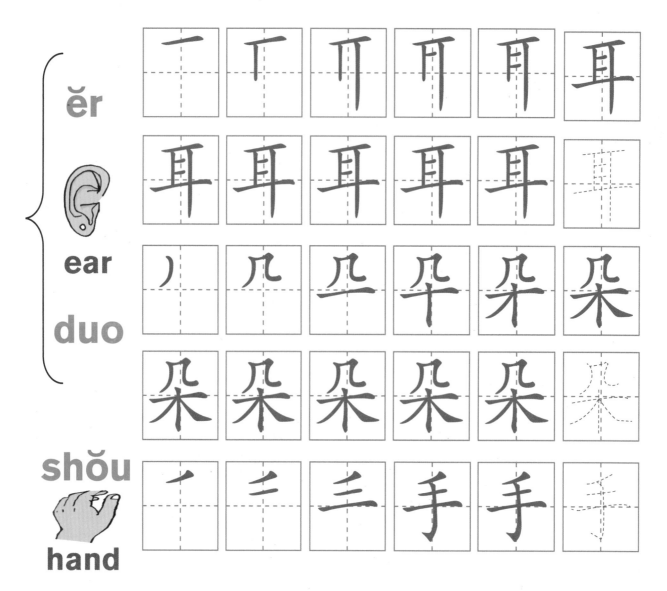

ěr

ear

duo

shǒu

hand

Hands are handy! Count how many Chinese characters there are for **hands** in the picture below!

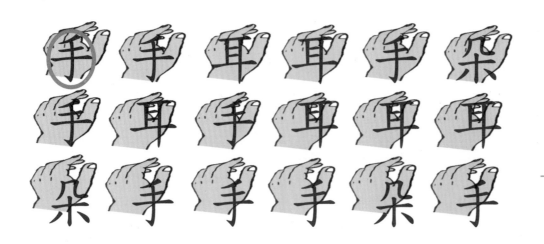

Answer

_____

Let's learn some Chinese characters for parts of the face and body!

yǎnjīng
眼睛

bízi
鼻子

zuǐba
嘴巴

jiǎo
脚

Help Dàlóng link the face and body parts to the Chinese characters!

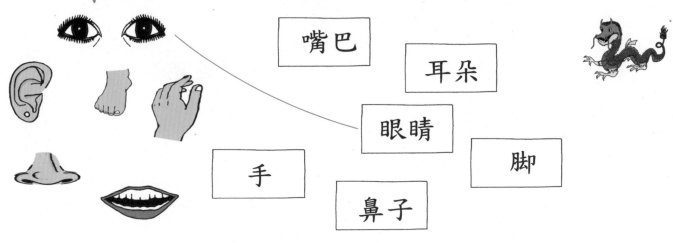

嘴巴

耳朵

眼睛

脚

手

鼻子

Xiǎolóng has lost some parts of his face. Fill in the missing Chinese characters!

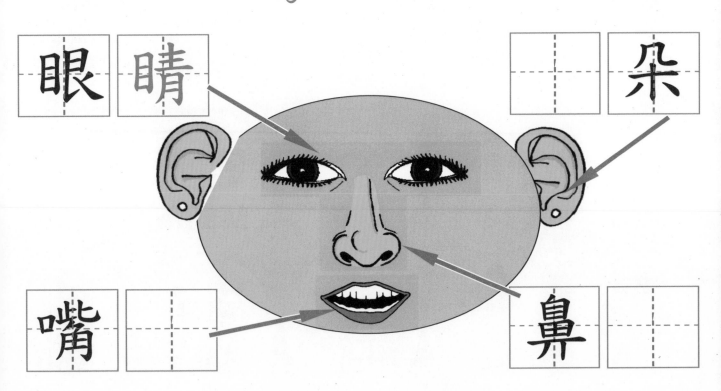

眼 睛

朵

嘴

鼻

What have you learnt in Chapter 8?

1	2	3	4	5
dà	shé	liù	mò	lù
mā	chē	jī	Fó	zhū
chá	èr	lí	bō	Měiguó
mǎ	è	mǐ	Māma	zhú
lǎoshī	kě	qì	Bàba	shǔ

Congratulations, you have completed Chapter 8

Your name: _____

Now I can...

 say *eyes*, *nose*, *ears* and *mouth* in Chinese.

 say *arm*, *hand*, *leg* and *foot* in Chinese.

 point to different parts of my body in Chinese.

 write *ear* and *hand* in Chinese characters.

 recognise *eye*, *nose*, *mouth* and *foot* in characters.

Let's go and learn more Chinese in Chapter 9!

11 and 12

shí	+	yī	11
shí	+	èr	12

1-6 o'clock

yī diǎn	1 o'clock
liǎng diǎn	2 o'clock
sān diǎn	3 o'clock
sì diǎn	4 o'clock
wǔ diǎn	5 o'clock
liù diǎn	6 o'clock

7-12 o'clock

qī diǎn	7 o'clock
bā diǎn	8 o'clock
jiǔ dian	9 o'clock
shí diǎn	10 o'clock
shí yī diǎn	11 o'clock
shí èr diǎn	12 o'clock

Jǐ diǎn le?	What time is it?
Sān diǎn le.	It's 3 o'clock.

Firstly, let's review our numbers 1-10!

1	**yī**	一	6	**liù**	六
2	**èr**	二	7	**qī**	七
3	**sān**	三	8	**bā**	八
4	**sì**	四	9	**jiǔ**	九
5	**wǔ**	五	10	**shí**	十

Let's learn how to say and write **11** and **12** in Chinese!

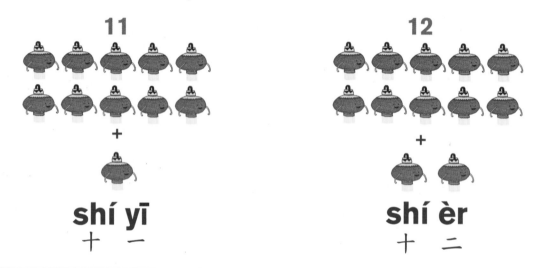

11

+

shí yī
十 一

12

+

shí èr
十 二

Help Candy match the Chinese numbers on the parcels to the Chinese characters on the houses!

Let's learn how to say 1, 2, 3, 4, 5, 6 o'clock in Chinese!

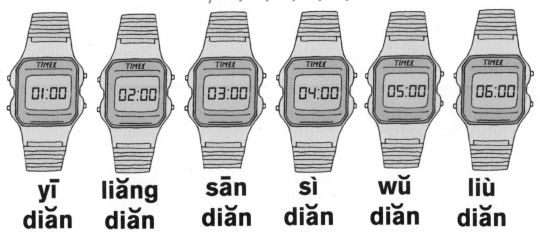

| yī diǎn | liǎng diǎn | sān diǎn | sì diǎn | wǔ diǎn | liù diǎn |

Let's learn how to say 7, 8, 9, 10, 11, 12 o'clock in Chinese!

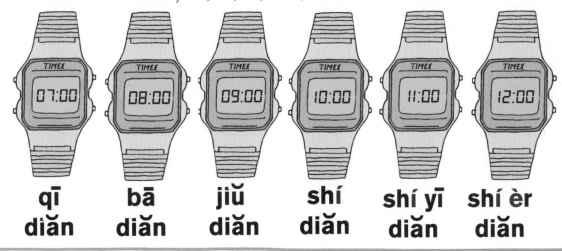

| qī diǎn | bā diǎn | jiǔ diǎn | shí diǎn | shí yī diǎn | shí èr diǎn |

Look at the clocks and then fill in the gaps in Chinese!

What time does Candy eat her supper?  __qī diǎn__

What time does Mike drink his tea?  _____

What time does Dàlóng eat breakfast? _____

What time does panda eat pizza? _____

How do you **ask the time** in Chinese?

Jǐ diǎn le?

What time is it?

What time is it? It's 12 o'clock!

Jǐ diǎn le?

Shí èr diǎn le.

What time is it?   **It's 12 o'clock.**

Complete the clock by writing the missing numbers from 1 to 12 in Chinese in the empty boxes!

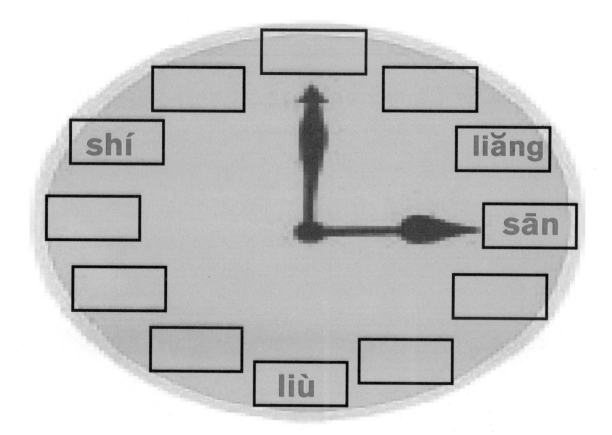

What time is it? It's 3 o'clock!

Jǐ diǎn le?

Sān diǎn le

What time is it?　　　　**It's 3 o'clock**

Candy is a horse! Which Chinese star sign are you?

The Animal Years

2001	2002	2003	2004	2005	2006
Snake	Horse	Goat	Monkey	Rooster	Dog
2007	2008	2009	2010	2011	2012
Pig	Rat	Ox	Tiger	Rabbit	Dragon

Let's tell the time using Chinese characters!

It's 2 o'clock

两 点 了

liǎng

2

一	丁	币	两	两	两
两	两	两	两	两	两

diǎn

丨	卜	卜	占	占	占
点	点	点	点	点	点

le

一	㇈	了	了	了	了

How many Chinese characters are there below?
Count them carefully and write the answers in Chinese!

一
两
点
了

一	二	三	四	五	一	一	一	六	七	八	一	一	六	七	七	liù
两	九	两	二	两	两	五	两	两	六	两	七	两	两	两	五	____
点	点	点	三	点	点	点	四	八	点	点	点	点	点	点	点	____
四	了	一	了	了	了	了	了	了	了	了	四	了	了	四	了	____

Trace over the numbers for 1-12 with your pen!

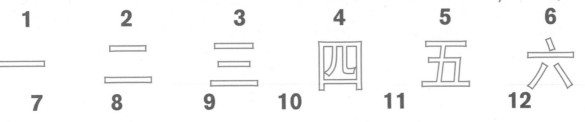

1　二　2　三　3　四　4　五　5　六　6

一　二　三　四　五　六

7　8　9　10　11　12

七　八　九　十　十一　十二

Help Candy to add up the Chinese characters! Fill in the answers in the boxes!

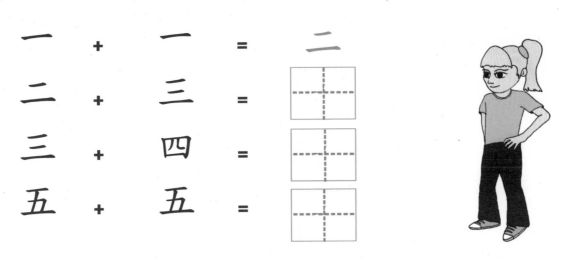

一　＋　一　＝　二

二　＋　三　＝　☐

三　＋　四　＝　☐

五　＋　五　＝　☐

It's **eight** o'clock. Write the time in Chinese characters!

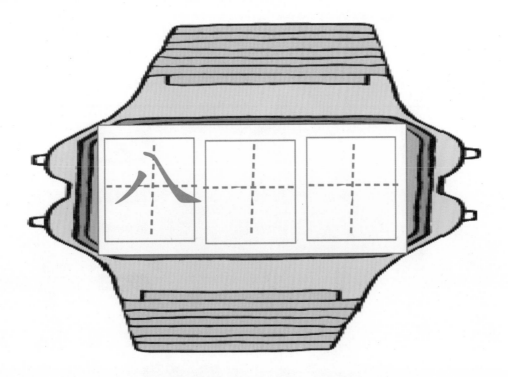

What have you learnt in Chapter 9?

1	2	3	4	5
dà	shé	liù	mò	lù
mā	chē	jī	Fó	zhū
chá	èr	lí	bō	Měiguó
mǎ	è	mǐ	Māma	zhú
lǎoshī	kě	qì	Bàba	shǔ

Match the correct stickers to the Chinese words!

6	7	8	9
hóng	hē	yǎnjīng	shí yī
shū	pīsà	bízi	sān diǎn
lán	chī	ěrduo	Jǐ diǎn le?
lǜ	shuǐ	zuǐba	jiǔ diǎn
bāo	kělè	shǒu	shí èr

Congratulations, you have completed Chapter 9

Your name: _____

Now I can...

 say numbers *11* and *12* in Chinese.

 ***ask the time* in Chinese.**

 ***tell the time* in Chinese.**

 say what my *Chinese animal year* is.

 write *2* and *o'clock* in Chinese characters.

Let's go and learn more Chinese in Chapter 10!

Top half

màozi	hat
chènshān	shirt
máoyī	jumper
jiákè	jacket

Bottom half

kùzi	trousers
qúnzi	skirt
wàzi	socks
xiézi	shoes

3 colours

huáng	yellow
hēi	black
bái	white

Nǐ chuān shénme? What are you wearing?

Wǒ chuān wàzi. I am wearing socks.

Let's learn some of our first words for clothes in Chinese

màozi  hat

chènshān  shirt

máoyī  jumper

jiákè jacket

Let's learn more words for clothes in Chinese!

kùzi   trousers

qúnzi  skirt

wàzi  socks

xiézi  shoes

Dàlóng has lost half of his clothes! Help him to link the 2 halves to make up full Chinese words!

mào

zi

zi

wà

zi

jiá

zi

shān

xié

qún

kù

kè

máo

chèn

zi

yī

Help Xiǎolóng to count his clothes in Chinese!

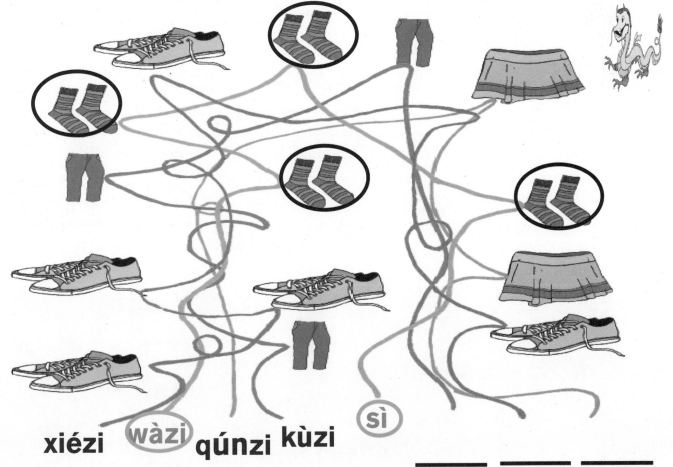

xiézi wàzi qúnzi kùzi sì

_____ _____ _____

Let's learn yellow, black and white in Chinese!

yellow huáng

black **hēi**

white **bái**

Do you remember the 3 colours we learnt in Chapter 6?

hóng red

lǜ green

lán blue

Circle the answer to each question.

What colour is a London bus?

(hóng)
lán

What colour is sunshine?

lǜ
huáng

What colour is a snowman?

hēi
bái

What colours are the Chinese flag?

huáng
hóng

How do you ask 'What are you wearing' in Chinese?

Nǐ chuān shénme?

What are you wearing?

How do you say 'I am wearing a jacket' in Chinese?

Wǒ chuān jiákè.

Wǒ chuān xiézi.

I am wearing a jacket. **I am wearing shoes.**

Colour my clothes! Match the clothes and the colours, then write the answers in English on the right!

	xiézi	qúnzi	kùzi	màozi	wàzi	**Answer**
hóng		X				**Red skirt**
huáng			X			____
lán	X					____
lǜ				X		____
hēi					X	____

Let's learn how to write some clothes in Chinese!

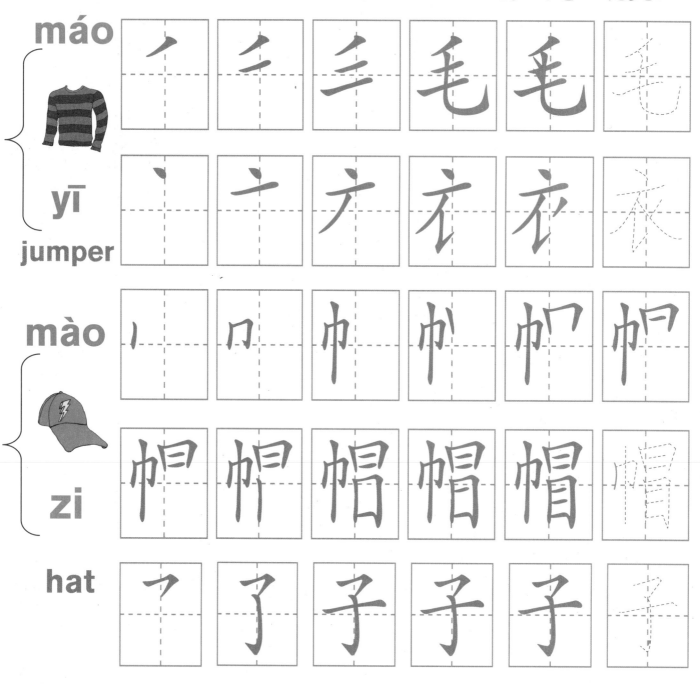

máo

yī

jumper

mào

zi

hat

It's cold! Mike wants to put his jumper and hat on. Can you help him complete the Chinese characters below?

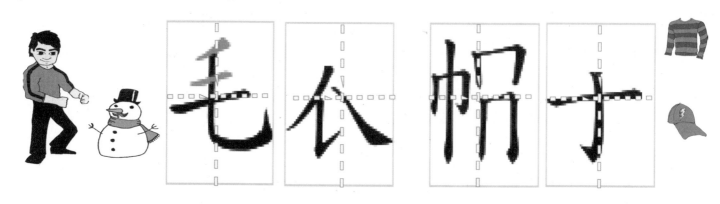

Let's see the Chinese characters for our 3 new colours!

huáng   hēi    bái

黄　　　黑　　　白

Help Candy match the colours to the Chinese characters. Look, we have done one for you!

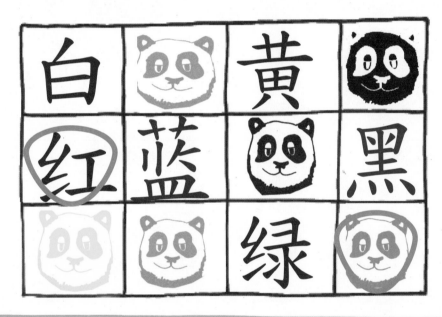

Look at the Chinese characters, then colour the flag!

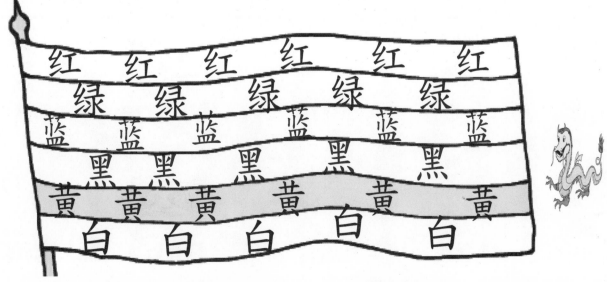

What have you learnt in Chapter 10?

1	2	3	4	5
dà	shé	liù	mò	lù
mā	chē	jī	Fó	zhū
chá	èr	lí	bō	Měiguó
mǎ	è	mǐ	Māma	zhú
lǎoshī	kě	qì	Bàba	shǔ

Match the correct stickers to the Chinese words!

6	7	8	9	10

hóng

hē

yǎnjīng

shí yī

màozi

shū

pīsà

bízi

sān diǎn

bái

lán

chī

ěrduo

Jǐ diǎn le?

màoyī

lǜ

shuǐ

zuǐba

jiǔ diǎn

hēi

bāo

kělè

shǒu

shí èr

huáng

Congratulations, you have completed Chapter 10.

Your name: _____

Now I can...

 say *hat, shirt, jumper* and *jacket* in Chinese.

 say *trousers, skirt, socks* and *shoes* in Chinese.

 say *what I am wearing* in Chinese.

 say *yellow, black* and *white in Chinese.*

 write *jumper* and *hat* in Chinese characters.

Congratulations, you have completed Book 1.

QUICK SEARCH

GREETINGS

nǐ hǎo	hello
zàijiàn	goodbye
xièxie	thank you
Nǐ hǎo ma?	How are you?
Wǒ hěn hǎo	I am well

NUMBERS

yī	1	**qī**	7
èr	2	**bā**	8
sān	3	**jiǔ**	9
sì	4	**shí**	10
wǔ	5	**shí yī**	11
liù	6	**shí èr**	12

MY FAMILY

Bàba	Dad
gēge	big brother
dìdi	little brother

Māma	Mum
jiějie	big sister
mèimei	little sister

COUNTRIES

Zhōngguó	China
Yīngguó	England
Měiguó	America
Fǎguó	France

CITIES

Lúndūn	London
Běijīng	Beijing

IN MY BAG

bāo	bag
shū	book
chǐ	ruler
bǐ	pen

THIS AND THAT

zhè	this
nà	that
zhè shì	this is
nà shì	that is

COLOURS

hóng	red
lǜ	green
lán	blue
huáng	yellow
hēi	black
bái	white

Food and Drink

chī	eat	hē	drink
nànbǎobāo	hamburger	shuǐ	water
miàntiáo	noodles	kělè	Coca Cola
pīsà	pizza	chá	tea

Parts of the Body

yǎnjīng	eye	gēbo	arm
bízi	nose	shǒu	hand
ěrduo	ear	jiǎo	foot
zuǐba	mouth	tuǐ	leg

Clothes

màozi	hat	kùzi	trousers
chènshān	shirt	qúnzi	skirt
máoyī	jumper	wàzi	socks
jiákè	jacket	xiézi	shoes

ANIMALS

jī	chicken
lù	deer
lóng	dragon
mǎ	horse
zhū	pig
shǔ	rat
shé	snake

USEFUL QUESTIONS

Nǐ jiào shénme?	What's your name?
Nǐ jǐ suì?	How old are you?
Nǐ zhù zài nǎlǐ?	Where do you live?
Jǐ diǎn le?	What time is it?

USEFUL ANSWERS

Wǒ jiào Max.	I am called Max.
Wǒ qī suì.	I am 7 years old.
Wǒ zhù zài Zhōngguó.	I live in China.
Liù diǎn le.	It's 6 o'clock.